GRAVITY, MAGICAL, MAGNETIC AND SPOOK HILLS AROUND THE WORLD

By

James Foster Robinson

(c) 2014
James Foster Robinson
West Virginia, USA

THANKS TO

My wife, Betty, for putting up with my puttering away on the computer, Createspace.com and Amazon.com for the opportunity to self publish my books, and the following people and organizations for permission to use their photos:

Tourism Moncton, NB, Canada

Burlington Historical Society, Ontario, Canada

Roberto Revelli, Professor of Hydraulics, Politecnio di Torino, Italy

Fulvio Rinaudo, Professor of Surveying, Politecnio di Torino, Italy

Mary and Angus Hogg at www.geograph.org.uk

Charles Schule at www.liminality.org/imagery/jeju2005/48/

Also thanks to my stepdaughter Taletha for telling me about the gravity hill in Logan, West Virginia

CONTENTS

INTRODUCTION

They stopped their car at the suggested spot, put it in neutral and were amazed when the car rolled slowly up the hill all by itself. Then they parked it, got out and poured a bottle of water on the road. Again, to their amazement, the water flowed up hill on the roadway. What was going on here? Was gravity reversed at this spot? There are a large number of such spots around the world. I have attempted to compile as many as I could find out about here in this guide. I have also listed some does and don'ts, which would be wise of you to follow if you are determined to try and test any of the mystical, magical, antigravity spots!

I researched the Internet and what others sources I was able to obtain. I found some confusion as to location of some sites and have tired to sort them out. If there are mistakes, duplications, etc, they are my fault. If you email me at jamesfosterrobinson@live.com with the correct information, I will make the corrections. This is possible as I publish this book and others on createspace.com in print on demand and digital platforms.

James Foster Robinson
May 2014
West Virginia

WHAT IS IT?

Wikipedia, the free encyclopedia online, defines a gravity hill, (magnetic hill, mystery hill, mystery spot, or gravity road) as a specific place at which the surrounding land layout produces an optical illusion where a very slight downhill slope appears to be an uphill slope. Thus, a car in neutral will seem to roll up hill against gravity. In bicycle racing, such spots are called as "false flats." These special spots are fairly common around the world. I have complied this guide and suggestions on how to SAFELY investigate and experience them for those interested in the phenomenon.

HOW DOES IT WORK?

It has been claimed that magnetic or even supernatural forces cause these phenomena at these spots. Many of the so-called gravity hills, etc., have legends attached to them claiming that one or more ghost push the vehicle up the supposed incline. But scientists have proved that most if not all such spots are the result of optical illusions.

There are several processes that help us to determine which way is up. There is a balance mechanism in our inner ears that keeps us from falling over. Visual clue are also a great aid but can in certain circumstances cause false perception. It is our false perception of a hill or slope that occurs at magnetic hills.

If the local horizon is fully or partially obscured and not actually level but tilted to some extent, this false horizon can cause us to perceive objects such as roads to be vertical, when in reality, they are not. Thus, what we see as an upwardly incline in the road may actually be a downward slope. A vehicle or other object will then appear to be rolling uphill when it is actually rolling down hill. Magnetic hills and such are simply optical illusions.

The false perception of optical illusion is similar to the well-known Ames room where balls appear to roll against gravity. Then there are special built rooms were one person looks through a window or doorway while watching another person walk into the room towards the back. The person in the room appears to grow taller to the surprise of the observer. This too is an optical illusion as the back of the room is actually smaller than the front thus making the person look taller. My son and I enjoyed this illusion when we visited the Ontario

Science Museum in Toronto, Ontario.

False perspective is another factor that can fool our sense of perspective such as where a row of trees get larger or smaller with distance. Thus such objects may seem larger or smaller than they ready are.

It is also easy to over estimate slope angles where a one degree slope appears to be five degrees and a five degree slope twenty degrees. Thus an antigravity illusion may appear to be stronger than it really is.

What it all boils down to is that these so-called anti-gravity hills are just optical illusions even the ones with legends of ghost pushing vehicles to safety.

METHODS OF TESTING

To test to see if there is really a magnetic anomaly, take two plumb lines to the site. One line should have a stone bob while the other an iron one. If there is a strong magnetic field acting horizontally on objects then the two plumb lines should hang at different angles. The stronger the magnetic force (such as one needed to pull a car up the supposed incline) would make the angle between the two plumb lines very significant. I grant you that there some known magnetic anomalies but they are not sufficiently strong to cause even a small metal ball to role up high.

Another method would be to place a carpenter's level of sufficient length to get a good reading on the supposed up hill slope. If the seeming upslope is true, then the bubble in level should be displaced to the upper end of the level tube. However, if it is in the lower end of the tube, then the supposed upslope is actually a down slope and hence the illusion that the object is rolling uphill.

If one were to look at a good topographical map of the area, it should show the way the land really slopes and that the supposed up slope is really sloping downward.

By now, you are wondering if it is really worth it to check this phenomenon out. By all means do so using the above mentioned techniques. If you do go out to a site, there are some precautions you should consider for your safety and others. Highway and local law may prohibit stooping or reversing your vehicle on bends, on and off ramps and slip roads.

SAFETY FIRST!

Remember that in most cases you will be on a public road and have to obey the traffic laws. Check with local law enforcement about rules and restrictions that may apply to the site you are visiting. The Magnetic Hill at Moncton, New Brunswick, Canada is apparently gated off and you have to pay a fee to visit the site. Be aware of traffic coming from both directions. DO NOT attempt to check out the site alone, at night or in bad weather. Always have someone there to watch for traffic, etc. And make sure that you or someone is in the driver's seat to control the car when it starts to roll by itself.

DOING THE TEST

It is simple. Stop your vehicle at the supposed bottom of the hill and put the car's gears in neutral. While remaining in the vehicle, take your foot off the brakes and enjoy the illusion of it rolling up hill. You can also pour water on the road or place a bottle on it and watch them flow supposedly uphill. You can try any number number of objects as long no one is endangered by them.

DIRECTORY OF MAGNETIC BY COUNTRIES

AUSTRALIA

BOWEN MOUNTAINS

A magnetic hill known as Magic Mountain and Richmond Magnetic Hill can be found on Bowen Mountain Road in the Township of Mountain Bowen in New South Wales, just east of Richmond at the intersection of Bowen Mountain Road and Westbury Road. The so-called magnetic effect only works apparently for fifty meters going up the hill.

MOONBI, NEW SOUTH WALES

A gravity hill is located near the Moonbi Lookout at the village of Moonbi on the New England Highway twenty kilometers north of Tamworth, New South Wales. Part of the Tamworth Regional Council Local Government Area, Moonbi is nestled at the foot of the Moonbi Range, a few kilometers north of Kootingal. At the village of Moonbi drive six kilometers up the 1st Moonbi Hill until you see a road that turns right at the foot of the Moonbi Park Lookout Road. This short road connects the northbound lane with the southbound lane and looks like it slopes from the northbound lane to the southbound lane.

ORROROO

Photo in public domain as per commons.wikimedia. org/wiki/File:Orroroo,_Magnetic_Hill.JPG

A Magnetic Hill can be found at Orroroo, a town in the Flinders Ranges region of South Australia. The hill was formerly named Bruff's Hill after a Mr. Bruff who had settled there in 1897. Local legend says that the magnetic properties of the hill were discovered by accident in the 1930's. A local man was driving his first auto on that road and got a flat on Bruff's Hill. Before jacking up the vehicle, he put a stone in front of the wheels to keep it from rolling downhill. Imagine his surprise when his new car started rolling UP hill! I hope he was able to stop it before any damage was done.

To get to the hill, drive out on the road from Peterborough towards Orroroo for about twenty-five kilometers until you come to a T- Junction. Here you turn left and drive for another kilometer to a railway crossing. About four hundred meters from the crossing you will see a gravel road with a sign reading "Magnetic Hill 8 kilometers". Follow the signs until you get to the hill where there should be a sign designating the spot to stop. Take all the necessary precautions mentioned earlier and enjoy the experience.

WOOD-END, VICTORIA

There is an anti-gravity hill, as they call it, on Straw Lane Road at Wood-End, Victoria and one hour drive up Calder Highway from Melbourne (seventy-seven kilometers). It is also near the infamous Hanging Rock which was the site of a mysterious missing persons case and the 1975 motion picture Picnic at Hanging Rock. Be aware that the Anti-Gravity Hill is not marked in any way and may be hard to find.

AZERBAIJAN

HANLAR

A magnetic hill exists a road on the way to Gek-Gek lake in western Azerbaijan, three miles (four and one-eight kilometers) from the town of Hanlar. While the locals knew about it, the spot only became widely known in the 1980's.

BARBADOS

MORGAN LEWIS HILL

There is a Magnetic hill at Morgan Lewis Hill in St Andrew, Barbados. Saint Andrew is one of eleven parishes of Barbados in the northern area in the country and has a number of rolling hills. I have found little information about the magnetic hill. and its exact location.

BRAZIL

BELO HORIZONTE

There is a magnetic hill on Rua do Amendoim, a street in the city of Belo Horizonte, the capital of the State of Minas Gerais, Brazil. Belo Horizonte is Portuguese for "Peanut Street". Brazilians believe peanuts can increase sexual prowess and help certain things to rise of their own accord. It is also believed that the large deposit of iron in the nearby cliff and mountain causes the magnetic effect.

Picture at worldofsupernatural.blogspot.com/2008/08/mystery -of-ladeira-do-amendoim-slope-of.html

CANADA

BRITISH COLUMBIA

ABBOTSFORD

A gravity or magnetic hill can be found on McKee Road apparently just before the Ledgeview Golf Course in Abbotsford, east of Vancouver. I have no further information on it.

MAPLE RIDGE

A magnetic hill is said to exist just east of Albion on Thornhill in the Whonock area. I lived in the Lower Mainland area of British Columbia but have not heard of this hill. However, they say you have to drive a bit south of 100th Ave. on 256th Street in the Maple Ridge Real Estate neighborhood. Stop at the bottom of a little dip just past a school. Stop your vehicle, check for traffic, put your vehicle in neutral and experience it apparently rolling up the dip.

There is a video at
www.youtube.com/watch?v=B1TXlVpuLOw.

VERNON

The city of Vernon lies just north of Kelowna in the interior of British Columbia. A magnetic hill is located on the Dixon Dam Road near Silver Star. If you can find the specific spot and follow the safety instructions given earlier, you will experience your vehicle appearing to roll uphill all by itself. It's geographical co-ordinates are 50°17'19"N 119°12'35"W.

MANITOBA

NEEPAWA

A magnetic hill is said to exist near Neepawa in Manitoba, but I have found no further information on it.

NOVA SCOTIA

BRIDGETOWN

A magnetic hill is located at Bridgetown, Nova Scotia on Hampton Mountain Road one kilometer (one mile) north of Valleyview Provincial Park. I have no further information concerning it.

NEW BRUNSWICK

MONCTON

**Moncton's Magnetic Hill road is to left in the back ground.
Used by permission of Tourism Moncton, NB, Canada**

The Magnetic Hill is just off the Trans Canada highway at the base of a ridge named "Lutes Mountain", that is several hundred feet above the Petitcodiac River valley near the city of Moncton.

Originally a cart path in the 19th century, it was developed into a regular road by the 1930's. Drivers of cars began to notice that while driving south at one point at the base of the ridge, they had to accelerate to keep from rolling backwards and were puzzled as this meant that the car was rolling backwards up the hill. That spot became known as "Magnetic Hill" and quickly became an popular attraction. When a "Mountain Road" bypass was built further west of Magnetic Hill, a one kilometer segment of the gravel road became a major tourist attraction. Today, you have to pay a fee to the enter that gravel road if you want to experience the phenomenon.

The Canadian singer, Stompin' Tom Connors, sang about Moncton's Magnetic Hill in his song "C-A-N-A-D-A". Another musical artist, Raffi, sang about the phenomenon on his Bananaphone album.

Vidoes on Youtube.com:
www.youtube.com/watch?v=Ml6E45x825M&feature=related
www.youtube.com/watch?v=JLgdZGbOclk
www.youtube.com/watch?v=zhr0owdDLqo&feature=related

ONTARIO

BURLINGTON

Bruce Filman, Photographer
Used by permission of the Burlington Historical Society, Ontario,
Canada

A magnetic hill can be found on Ontario's King Road at Burlington just north of Bayview Park near the village of Aldershot at geographic co-ordinates of Latitude 43.37, Longitude -79.814166. King Road runs from Burlington Bay to the top of the Niagara Escarpment. The Magnetic Hill is just four kilometers from downtown Burlington. Once known as the 'Dump' Road because the Burlington Landfill Site used to be located there, it was renamed King Road when the dump closed in 1988.

Some people, who have tried the hill have reported failure of their cars, radios and electronic gadgets at that spot. Some have also reported felling strange electrical pulses like they were getting a small shock as well as numbness in their hands and arms. Strange noises, such as the sounds of horses and wagons, were also reported as well as ghosts who appear to be long passed away pioneers. They carried old fashioned guns while walking through the fields in the area. Pictures have been taken showing faded images of figures in the woods and along the road.

CALEDON

There is supposedly a magnetic or gravity hill at or near Caledon on the Escarpment Sideroad approaching Highway 10. Look for a tunnel and stop there. No other information is available at this time.

A video can be found at
www.youtube.com/watch?v=z6ayPND6UVk

DACRE

Dacre's Magnetic Hill lies at Tooey's Hill on an old section of Highway 41 near the intersection with Highway 132. The phenomenon existed until the 1980's when the forest grew and occurred the false horizon that created the illusion. That section of the road is no longer used and the woods is gradually taking it over also.

SPARTA

A magnetic hill is said to exist on Centennial Avenue near the town of Sparta near St. Thomas. To get to it (if the information I found is correct) follow old Highway 4 south towards Port Stanley, turning left at Union onto County Road #27 towards Sparta. Go about three kilometers down the road until you see an old school and a small cemetery at an intersection with Centennial Road. Turn left here and head north on Centennial for nearly a kilometer until you come to a steep slope. This should be the Magnetic Hill. There is also mention of a magnetic hill being on Yarmouth Centre Road between Sparta Line (Highway 27) and Fruit Ridge Line, facing south. This may be the same one on Centennial Avenue.

QUEBEC

CHARTIERVILLE

Picture by David W brooks and is available under the Creative Commons CC0 1.0 Universal Public Domain Dedication

A Magnetic Hill is said to be in Chartierville, Quebec on Route 257, south of La Patrie and on quarter mile from the New Hampshire border. A bi-lingual sign explains how you can experience the phenomenon.

A map can be found on the Internet at www.roadsideamerica. com/map/14577

Videos on youtube:

www.youtube.com/watch?v=V56rYBMr_vg

www.youtube.com/watch?v=Uo_wzq_SCwc

CZECH REPUBLIC

MORAVSKA TREBOVA

A magnetic hill can be found near Moravska Trebova in the Czech Republic on a one way road to Borsov running down hill. To get to it take Road E442 about six kilometers from Moravska Trebova towards Svitavy and turn down that road to Borsov. Remember it is a one way road (they say) but I am not sure which way the one way is. Presumably from E442 to Svitavy.

It geographic co-ordinates are N 49° 45.140 E 016° 35.755

Video may be available at

www.youtube.com/watch?v=KsD8Fvwe92M

www.youtube.com/watch?v=ba4BpZHyzhg.

CHINA

GANSU

A magnetic hill with a two hundred feet (sixty-one meters) slope at an angle of fifteen degrees is said to be in a desert region of Yugur County near Gansu, China. No further information is available at this time.

SHENYANG

Shenyang, the largest city in Northeast China, is the capital of Liaoning Province. A magnetic hill called the Strange Slope (Guaipo), which is more than eighty meters (about 87.5 yards) long is located near there. Drivers and bike riders have had to accelerate to go down the hill but could easily roll back up the slope. Obviously the slope is an optical illusion.

DOMINICAN REPUBLIC

POLO

Polo, a municipality of the Barahona Province in southwestern Dominican Republic, also has El Polo Magnético (the magnetic pole), a spot on a nearby mountain.

A video is available on youtube at
www.youtube.com/watch?v=hmy7RNR824c

FRANCE

LAURIOLE

La Curiosité de Lauriole can be found near the small town of Lauriole, six kilometers west of Minerve and thirty kilometers north-east of Carcassonne.

Pictures at www.odeaanaude.eu/catalog/-p-663.html

A picture of the road sign pointing to the site is available at s1107.photobucket.com/user/bev9219/media/South of France 2011/Picture038.jpg.html

Videos in French are available at
www.youtube.com/watch?v=xrf1LMMBYDo
www.youtube.com/watch?v=Uq6BfTeKbCM

LES NOLES

Route Magique or Magical Road near the the village Les

Noës is a three hundred meter road between La Loge des Gardes and Renaison where the optical illusion of gravity appears to be reversed. It is of course a magnetic road.

GERMANY

BUTZBZACH

A gravity or magnetic road can be found on the L3053 between and Hausen-Oes.

GREECE

CEPHALONIA

Another magnetic spot is said to occur on the coastal road between Simotata and Platie on the Greek island of Cephalonia.

MOUNT PENTELI

Drivers on the road to Mount Penteli, Athens, can experience the seemingly reversal of gravity at the magnetic spot. Magnetic abnormalities have been recorded on the road from Penteli to Nea Makri and are said by some to explain the

Magnetic Hill effect there.

A video about the "Magic Mountain" in Greece is avalable at www.youtube. com/watch?v=U9_Q33sGB4U&feature=related

GREAT BRITAIN/UNITED KINGDOM

ENGLAND

ASTON CLINTON

You can find a magnetic hill off B4009 on Dancer's Lane in Aston Clinton, Buckinghamshire. Its GPS coordinates are N 51° 47.184 W 000° 41.646 48.

There may be another magnetic hill on the outskirts of Aston Clinton, Aylesbury, as its coordinates are given as N 51° 47.526 W 000° 41.915 which is different than the coordinates given for the one on Dancer's Lane.

BRISTOL

A steep hill near Tog Hill at Bristol (it might even be on Tog Hill) is said to be another magnetic or gravity hill.

A video is available at

www.youtube.com/watch?v=wF_fTnleS00&feature=related

EPPING FOREST

Hangman's Hill in Essex is not only haunted by a man and terrible screams have been heard, but there is also a magnetic hill where your car will appear to roll upwards towards the tree where people have been hanged.

Video is availabe

www.youtube.com/watch?v=9di6MnndLfU

ISLE OF MAN

A magnetic hill, between Ballabeg and the Round Table on the coastal road A7 on the Isle of Man, is another example of the optical illusion. But locals claim that it is not an optical illusion or a magnetic effect but the shenanigans of the Little People who are pushing the vehicles up that hill.

A map can be found at www.google. com/maps/place/Ballabeg/@54.1001735,-4.680794, 15z/data=!3m1!4b1!4m2!3m1!1s0x48638c8a7f260a83: 0x570fca6f66bc7ad1

There is a possible second hill at the bottom of a spot called the Sloc on A27. Drive A27 from Barrule until you see an almost hairpin turn. Once past that you are on part of the road that seems to slope upwards. This should be it.

Videos are found at
www.youtube.com/watch?v=UbUmOxytkZo
www.youtube.com/watch?v=9tNyPgLIUh4
www.youtube.com/watch?v=l_Ewl43YO5k&feature=related

ISLE OF WIGHT

The Isle of Wight has at least two magnetic hills of which one is possibly on the A3055 between Shanklin and Ventnor.

ROGATE

A magnetic hill can found on the A272 road seven miles west of Rogate, a village in the Chichester district of West Sussex in the Western Rother valley. No further information is available at this time.

WARBOYS

There is a spook or ghost hill near Warboys, Cambridgeshire. According to local legend, a school bus wrecked on the train tracks and all the children were killed. Now the ghosts of the children try to push your vehicle to safety. Drive through Warboys on High Street until you come to Station Road. Take it out of the village until you come to the signs for the village and then turn right onto "Spooks Hill". Look for a humpback bridge at the top of the hill. You should be there or quite near it. Good Luck!

Youtube videos:
www.youtube.com/watch?v=881vJi2H3yo
www.youtube.com/watch?v=7ByJ24XMvZk&feature=related

YETMINSTER

There is a report of a magnetic hill near Yetminster in Dorset but I have not been able to find anything about it.

SCOTLAND

ELECTRIC BRAE

Electric Brae aka Croy Brae
Used with permission of Mary and Angus Hogg www.geograph.org.uk

The Electric Brae in South Ayrshire, whose real name is Croy Brae, on the A719   approximately three miles (5 kilometers) northwest of Maybole and a mile (1.5 kilometers) south of Dunure near Croy Bay, South of Ayr, Ayeshire. It gets it name from the optical illusion of a car rolling up a hill by itself. It was suggested that electrical forces were the cause and thus the name was born. There is a layby at the side of the road where you can experience the phenomenon. There is a stone slab, often called a cairn, in the layby which has the inscription:

"The 'Electric Brae', known locally as Croy Brae.

This runs the quarter mile from the bend overlooking Croy railway viaduct in the west (286 feet Above Ordnance Datum) to the wooded Craigencroy Glen (303 feet above A.O .D.) to the east.

Whilst there is this slope of 1 In 86 upwards from the bend at the Glen, the configuration of the land on either side of the road provides an optical illusion making it look as if the slope is going the other way.

Therefore, a stationary car on the road with the brakes off will appear to move slowly uphill.

The term 'Electric Brae' dates from a time when it was incorrectly thought to be a phenomenon caused by electric or magnetic attraction within the Brae."

Videos on the Electric Brae can be found at

www.youtube.com/watch?v=MRuEUSiMalk

www.youtube.com/watch?v=AofTlPpCIxQ

www.youtube.
com/watch?v=DBSRLtLBvpA&feature=related

www.youtube.com/watch?v=JDhLTozHXlI&feature=related

www.youtube.com/watch?v=DsxrAGGcauk&feature=related

www.youtube.com/watch?v=5w8dMeysxaY&feature=related

NORTHERN IRELAND

B27

A magnetic hill is said to exist south east near the Spelga Dam on B27 in the Mourne Mountains in County Down. To get to the location follow the signs or get directions to the Spelga Dam. At a hair-pin turn, you will see the dam. Proceed until you are about one hundred meters before the dam. There go down a small road and stop at a small stone building another hundred meters. This is the spot.

Videos at

www.youtube.com/watch?v=mxTOiylFLB8&feature=related

www.youtube.com/watch?v=QR_GPXunr1s&NR=1

GUATEMALA

PASO MISTERIOSO (MYSTERY OF EL PASO)

The Mystery of El Paso is a magnetic hill about one hundred and thirty kilometers (eight-one miles) from the capital city of Guatemala on the road from Cocales, Suchitepequez Department to San Lucas Tolimán, Sololá .

The effect lasts for about two hundred meters. Locals believe that the rare stones such as gold and even deposits of oil beneath the surface cause the phenomenon. There are apparently two ways to get to it. Take the road from Panajachel to Godinez and then to the coast, looking for the sign that tell the spot. You can also go on the road to the south coast to the Cocales crossroad at kilometer 113. There take the road to Patulul but go another 18 kilometers until you see the sign for the Paso misterioso.

There are videos on Youtube at

www.youtube.com/watch?v=3E-fvs9huIM

www.youtube.com/watch?v=XFqsdpCB-O8&feature=related

INDIA

LEH

Photo by Gangadhar Tambe and is in the public domain as per en.wikipedia.org/wiki/File:Ladakh_-_Magnetic_Hill.jpg

The "magnetic hill" lies on the Leh-Kargil-Srinagar national highway, about fifty kilometers from Leh. Vehicles appear to roll up the slope at a speed of twenty kilometers/ hour with the gear in neutral. It is claimed that its magnetic properties are strong enough to cause passing planes to fly higher to escape its magnetic interference. A bill board has been set up to help tourists find the Magnetic Hill.

Images available at

ankurlearningsolutions.files.wordpress.com/2013/11/image1.jpg

ankurlearningsolutions.files.wordpress.com/2013/11/image2.jpg

ankurlearningsolutions.files.wordpress.com/2013/11/image3.jpg

ankurlearningsolutions.files.wordpress.com/2013/11/image4.jpg

ankurlearningsolutions.files.wordpress.com/2013/11/image5.jpg

ankurlearningsolutions.files.wordpress.com/2013/11/image6.jpg

en.wikipedia.org/wiki/FileLadakh_-_Magnetic_Hill_1.jpg

Video at

www.youtube.com/watch?v=C7xP09iuZh0&NR=1

INDONESIA

LIMPAKUWUS

A magnetic hill lies in Limpakuwus Village, District Contribute, Banyumas, Central Java, near the Center for Dairy Cattle Breeding. The effect apparently lasts for about two hundred meters.

Youtube videos are at

www.youtube.com/watch?v=xbhKDHB_-mE
www.youtube.com/watch?v=2irs7OBl4OE
www.youtube.com/watch?v=GAi9SZKzYJk

IRELAND

JENKINSTOWN

A Gravity Hill at Jenkinstown north of Dundalk in the Cooley Peninsula in County Louth is known as Magic Hill or Magic Road. It is located about seven miles on the road to Carlington north of Dundalk. Stop at a sign for McCrystals shop and some gas (petrol) pumps, and ask for directions in the shop. Local legend claims that the phenomena is caused by magic, invisible Leprechauns pulling the vehicles or a powerful magnetic force under the road. Andrew McCarthy, American actor and TV Presenter, featured the Magic Road on his TV show.

Video are apparently available at

irelandseden.ie/explore-eden/carlingford-the-cooley-peninsula/local-stories-and-traditions/the-magic-hill-jenkinstown-co-louth/

www.youtube.com/watch?v=k76ik_y0PJ4&NR=1

There is another "Magic Hill" on the road to Mahon Falls, Comeragh Mountains, County Waterford about ten miles north from Dungarvan on the coast. Look for a Wishing Tree or May Bush on the left when you crest a hill and head down into a small valley. Stop at the bush and this should be the spot. Put your vehicle in neutral and it should roll up the hill. The words "Magic Road" are supposed to be carved on a rock there. Local legend claims that people have trespassed in these spots on fairy land and the Fey do not like it. The Fey have supposedly cursed the Mahon Falls spot when the road was built through the area. The curse causes everything to go in reverse. Another explanation claims that a huge seam of copper lies under the road at the spot and, of course, is the reason for vehicles backing up the hill with out using the motor.

Videos available at

atriptoireland.com/2013/03/21/the-magic-roads-of-ireland/

There are said to be two more gravity hills. One is at Slievenamon near Clonmel, Co. Tipperary. The other might be found on Clogheen Road close to the car park near the right turn for Ardfinnan on the County Tipperary side of the Vee, a V-shaped turn on the road, in the Knockilometersealdown Mountains.

ITALY

ARICCIA

The "Ariccia' Downhill" lies between Albano and Nemi Lakes near Rome. If you drive from Rocca di Papa, a little town near Rome, toward Ariccia, you apparently cross the "via dei laghi" and get on the SS218. After about one hundred meters you will find the "magic downhill" or

"Ariccia' Downhill". The CICAP Lazio ('Italian Committee for the Investigation of Claims of the Paranormal', section of Rome) did an investigation of the phenomenon in February 2009 and confirmed it was an optic illusion.

COLLI ALBANI

There is supposed to be another magnetic hill south of Rome, in Colli Albani, near Frascati, Italy. I have not been able to confirm it at the time of writing.

MENFI

Another mystery road is said to be just north of Menfi, a commune in the Agrigento Province in Sicily, seventy kilometers southwest of Palermo and about sixty kilometers northwest of Agrigento. Once again, I can not find any further information on it at the time of writing.

MONTAGNAGA

The "mirage" slope in Montagnaga can be found near the entrance to the community. It appears at first to be a down slope but if you stop your car at the stop signal and put it in neutral, it will start to roll back up the slope almost all the way to the town's sign post. It is of course an optical illusion and you are actually rolling down a down slope instead of up the slope. Sorry to ruin your fun.

Videos are at

www.youtube.com/watch?v=mg5ZcDbWBiM

www.youtube.com/watch?v=ykFqb5shvSs

Pictures available for viewing at

www.fabiovassallo.it/eng/cembravalley/montagnaga.html

ROCCABRUNA

Photo courtesy of Roberto Revelli, Professor of Hydraulics, Politecnio di Torino, Italy and Fulvio Rinaudo, Professor of Surveying, Politecnio di Torino, Italy

There is a "Down Hill" or gravity hill at Roccabruna in Cuneo Province in the Piedmont region, about seventy kilometers southwest of Turin and twenty kilometers northwest of

Cuneo. It slopes for about twenty meters near a humpback on the road that goes to the village of Roquebruna. Roberto Revelli (on the left in the photo above) and Fulvio Rinaudo (on the right) investigated the "Down Hill" and determined it is an optical illusion.

KENYA

MACHAKOS

Kituluni Hill, a few kilometers between Machakos and Kangundo in the Mua Hills is said to be another magnetic hill. It was discovered in colonial days when a colonist stopped his car on the hill to get some water from a nearby stream to cool his radiator. Imagine his surprise when his vehicle had some how rolled up the hill from the spot where he had left it. It seems he had left the hand brake off and it apparently had rolled all by itself. The spot quickly became a tourist attraction.

Video at
www.youtube.com/watch?v=e2hAiM2yjso&NR=
www.youtube.com/watch?v=MxXrHYnyTkilometers
www.youtube.com/watch?v=yRvjm6Wncw0

www.youtube.com/watch?v=e2hAiM2yjso&NR=

LEBANON

HAMAT

The Magical Miracle Road was discovered in the early 1990's in Hamat Lebanon and goes up the hill to the Lady of Nouriyeh, a convent built in 300 A.D. Some people believe it is a miracle from Saydet el Nourieh Diety. There is apparently no sign to indicate the phenomenon. But on one website, it advised the driver to take the main road to Chekka but turn right at the sign to Hamat. It also advises to view the picture at www.fanoos.com/reports/hamat_lebanon.html so that you will know what to look for.

A video can be viewed at
www.youtube.com/watch?v=ZlbkpYoIyrE

MALAYSIA

KIMANIS-KENINGAU HIGHWAY

A magnetic or mystery hill is located about eleven kilometers from Keningau on the Kimanis-Keningau Highway in Sabah, Malaysia.

Video on youtube.com at

www.youtube.com/watch?v=3pSpdZel24k

www.youtube.com/watch?v=Mlvsjxh5QKE

MOLDVO

ORHEI

Another mystery hill exists just outside Orhei Vechi just south of the city of Orhei. During World War II, the Nazis were said to have buried Jewish prisoners alive there. Now mysterious happenings occur at this site. One of there strange happening is the apparent reversal of gravity. If you park your car in the Safari Cafe lot facing the hill, put it in neutral, it will roll slowly a ways up the incline.

Video at

www.youtube.com/watch?v=gVwJbPMkRAc

killingbatteries.com/2010/06/the-legend-of-magnetic-hill-orhei-moldova/

romaniaandmoldova.com/moldova/orheiul-vechi/

OMAN

MIRBAT

An Anti-Gravity Point (Magnetic Hill) can be experienced at Mirbat about forty kilometers east of the coastal City of Salalah in the south of Oman. The country of Oman is on the southeast coast of the Arabian Peninsula.

Videos at
www.youtube.com/watch?v=JZpH_MAV4BE
www.youtube.com/watch?v=m5MXAyJs7XQ
vrakeshkumar.wordpress.com/tag/anti-gravity-road-magnetic-road-mirbat-salalah-oman/

PHILIPPINES

LOS BANOS

A Magnetic Hill can be found near the Boy Scouts Jamboree near the University of the Philippines in Los Baños Laguna just south of Calamba on the South Luzon Expressway. It is on a short stretch of road by a large property with metal gates on the left.

Videos at
www.youtube.com/watch?v=deR6oEEVfB8

Photos are at
www.eureka4you.com/magnetichillworldwide/LosBanos-LA.htm

eagronfiles.wordpress.com/2011/03/08/los-banos-magnetic-hill-truth-or-simply-an-optical-illusion/

MARIVELES

There is reported to be a reverse gravity slope on a road to MAAP in Marina Beach in Bataan in the Philippines.

Video at

www.youtube.com/watch?v=EU1BpK9WGds

POLAND

OPAWICA ROAD

A magnetic hill on the Opawica Road in south Poland has been listed in a number of lists of Reverse Phenomena but I have not been able to find any more information on it at the time of writing.

PORTUGAL

MALVEIRA DA SERRA

There is a gravity hill on a hill on coastal road N247 in Cascais near Malveira da Serra and Guincho Beach, west of Lisbon, Portugal.

Another hill is said to exist near Porto which is on the west coast. It may be in fact the same gravity hill mentioned above.

ROMANIA

CAVNIC

Varfu Hill lies on the road between Cavnic and Budeşti in Maramureş County. Its co-ordinates are 47.70469 N, 23,.1786 E. Little else is known about it.

A video is at www.orasulcavnic.ro/imprejurimi.html

SAUDI ARABIA

WADI AL JINN (VALLEY OF JINNS)

The Magnet or Gravity Hill of Madinah is said to be located in Wadi al Jinn (Valley of Jinns) at Madinah. Please note that this Holy City is often spelled as Medina or Madina. The correct spelling is apparently Madinah Al-Munawarrah or Madinah for short. Wadi al Jinn, also known as Wadi-E-Baida, Wadi-e-Al-Baida or Jabal Baido, is about thirty-seven miles (sixty kilometers) north west of Madinah.

Its coordinates are 24°43'21"N 39°26'35"E

There is a picture of the site at greatstuff.hubpages.com/hub/Magnetic-Hill-or-Magnet-Mountain-or-Gravity-Hill-in-Al-Madinah-Medina-Saudi-Arabia

SERBIA

IVANJE

A magnetic hill exists in the village of Ivanje (Midsummer) on Radan Mountain near Kursumlija. The effect is said to last about a hundred meters is is thought to be associated with Devil's Town of which many legends are told. It is a natural monument in southern Serbia.

Pictures of Devil's Town can be found at voiceofserbia.org/serbia/node/97

SOUTH AFRICA

PAREL VALLEI

Another gravity or magnetic hill exists between Greytown and Weenen, KwaZulu-Natal on the Cape Town Parel Vallei road, Parel Vallei, Somerset West. Look for a farm entrance about one hundred meters at the top of a straight road.

SOUTH KOREA

JEJU

Photo courtesy of Charles Schule at www.liminality. org/imagery/jeju2005/48/

The "Mysterious Road" also known as Dokkaebi Road that connects two major highways on Jejudo Island lies on a hill at the foot of a mountain.

Pictures at

english.visitkorea.or.kr/enu/SI/SI_EN_3_1_1_1.
jsp?cid=1373714

en.wikipedia.org/wiki/Jeju_Island

Video at   www.youtube.com/watch?v=trErzkq20xs

TAIWAN

TAITUNG

There is a small mystery spot just off the highway north of Taitung.

Video on Youtube
www.youtube.com/watch?v=i3PUxcSBn64&feature=related

THAILAND

A magnetic hill is in west Thailand but I can not find its location or any information on it.

A video on it can be found at
www.youtube.com/watch?v=-oNqEiIkZb8&feature=related

TURKEY

A magnetic hill is listed on a number of sites as being on the Pinarhisar-Demirköy Highway in Turkey but no details are given.

USA

ALASKA

ANCHORAGE

A magnetic hill may be found on the Upper Huffman Road, Hillside in Anchorage. According to the directions I found, you take the main highway out of Anchorage to the Seward Highway O'Malley exit. Take a right on Hill Side Drive just before you get to the top. Turn left onto Upper Huffman Rd. Drive when you have gone about a mile down the road to the top of the first hill and down the other side to the bottom, you should be there.

ALABAMA

HUNTSVILLE

Once again, I find only a mention and not details for Ghost Hill, supposedly a magnetic hill off Woodward Ave., Huntsville.

OAK GROVE

There is a gravity hill on "Gravity Hill Road (the old Highway 280) in the western part of Oak Grove just off Highway 280 in Talladega County toward Childerburg.

SYLACAUGA

Now there is a bit more information on a gravity hill at 117 Gravity Hill Lane north west of Sylacauga,. Go west right off Highway 53/280 at the top of the hill west of Fulton Gap Road to get to Gravity Hill Lane. It is reportedly next to a trailer on cylinder blocks. Let me know if these directions are not correct. Also this appears to be near Oak Grove and may be the same hill.

There is a map of the location at
www.roadsideamerica.com/map/3300

ARIZONA

A video of a gravity hill somewhere in Arizona is on www.youtube.com/watch?v=TZ75AlHh3i8

ARKANSAS

ALMA

Local Native Americans say there is a gravity hill at Alma Place near Alma. I have not been able to find any further information.

A video showing several sights and the gravity hill at Alma can be viewed at www.youtube.com/watch?v=QVbiI4PJS3U

DYER

An overpass at at the corner of Ridge Road and Melody Lane that goes over Interstate 40 is known as a gravity hill. It is not far from the old Alamo compound. A local legend claims that the cars are being pushed up the hill by the ghosts of a football team killed in a crash on I-40. Others feel it is the ghost of Susan Alamo.

Video at

5newsonline.com/2012/10/23/haunted-arkansas-gravity-hill/

www.youtube.com/watch?v=UEEgCLVePyc

HELENA

There is a gravity hill off Sulphur Spring Road, Helena. Drive on Route 185 and get off at Sulphur Springs Road. When you come to a stop sign, you are at the spot. Put your car in neutral and your car should start rolling by its self up the hill for about fifty yards.

Map at www.eureka4you.com/magnetichillworldwide/Helena -AR.htm

CALIFORNIA

ALTADENA

Altadena is a small community in Los Angeles County. The Angeles National Forest, aka The Haunted Forest (Cobb Estate), at the top of Lake Avenue has been the scene of strange unexplained screams and lights. Gravity Hill on Loma Alta Street in Altadena is supposedly haunted by three young kids who took a parent's car for a joy ride and were killed in an accident. Now if you park your car at the bottom of the hill, it is said that the dead kids will push it up the hill. People have also reported finding fingerprints on their cars after being pushed up the hill. I wonder if anyone took prints and checked them against the prints from the dead kids?

A different story claims that an elder Native American died when his wagon crashed after rolling out of control down the hill to a bridge. Now his spirit supposedly pulls (not pushes) cars up the hill to avoid his fate.

To get to Altadena's gravity hill drive north on Lake Avenue from Highway 210 in Pasadena. Take a right at Altadena Drive and then a left on Porter. Follow it to where it ends on East Loma Alta Drive and take a left on Loma Alta. After going around a few corners and through a few dips, you should find a hill with two Sonnyoaks signs. Stop at the second sign and you should be at the spot.

Videos at
www.youtube.com/watch?v=0Qscv5ei29Q&NR=1
www.youtube.com/watch?v=0Qscv5ei29Q&NR=1(ii)

www.youtube.com/watch?v=x4xKPCGtn_w&feature=related

ANTIOCH

A gravity hill on Empire road in the community of Antioch has two slightly different versions of why cars seemingly roll up the hill by themselves. The ghosts of children who drowned when their bus skidded off the road are the cause of the phenomenon. The other version says that the kids were killed by an escaped lunatic from the nearby and now closed asylum.

I found two sets of directions to Antioch's Gravity Hill. If you try them let me know if either one or both are accurate.

If you are coming from the eats or west, exit Highway 4 at Lone Tree Way and then turn right on Deer Valley Road. Then you take a right on Empire Road. If you are coming from the south, take Ygnacio Valley Road and then right on Clayton Road. Clayton Road turns into Marsh Creek Road. Next take a left on Deer Valley and a final left on Empire Mine Road.

BRENTWOOD

The gravity hill in Brentwood is a city in Contra Costa County is the subject of another classic urban legend. In the 1950 's, a bus load of children skidded off a road into water. All children drowned. Now they push cars placed to safety on the nearby road.

CABAZON

There is a magnetic hill on the Morongo Indian Reservation near Cabazon is in Riverside County. If you park at the bottom and it will roll steadily uphill.

CORONA

Corona is a city in Riverside County. The gravity hill there, now apparently leveled and paved recently, was supposedly haunted by the ghost of a distraught girl who crashed her car and died while driving fast on Lichau Road after an argument with her boyfriend. Her car wrecked when it hit a bump at the bottom of the hill. If you stop there and put your vehicle in neutral, she will push your car up the hill past the site where she crashed. Local legends also claims that she even leaves hand prints on your trunk (if it is dirty and you have not washed it lately).

GPS: 33.831001, -117.613869

DEVOURE

A gravity point or road can be found on Glen Helen Road in the community of Devoure. I am not sure where you start but they say that you have to drive over three sets of railroad tracks until you see a stop sign about one hundred feet beyond the third crossing. There should be a line just pass at the stop sign where you stop and put your vehicle in neutral. Other instructions say to " make a U-Turn and head back towards the tracks, but stop the car at the beginning of a chain link fence on the left hand (driver) side." Watch out for other traffic when you car starts to roll uphill by itself.

JACUMBA HOT SPRINGS

Jacumba Hot Springs is in the Mountain Empire area of southeastern San Diego County. There is a gravity hill there on In-Ko-Pah Road off of Interstate 8, west of Ocotillo near the Desert View Tower.

JAMUL

Jamul, a San Diego suburb, has its own gravity hill at an unspecified train track crossing. In the 1950's, a school bus full of children stalled on the tracks and was hit by an on coming train. They say your can hear the children screaming if you park on the tracks. Watch for trains or you may be the one screaming. And the ghosts of these children are said to push cars on the tracks to safety.

LA JOLLA

The La Jolla haunted hill can be found on West Muirlands Drive between Nautilus and Fay Streets. Drive down Nautilus to Fay Street until you see West Muirlands Drive and turn on to it. Stop at the pole with three yellow stripes on it by the fairway and the railway tracks that may or may not still be there. This should be the spot. The ghost of people killed when a train hit a stalled car on those tracks apparently try to push any vehicle to safety that stops in that area.

LIVEMORE

The gravity hill at Mile Marker 157 on Patterson Pass Road in Livermore, a city in Alameda County on the eastern edge of California's San Francisco Bay Area, has a different twist to the stories told about it. As your car is pushed uphill by ghosts, you can hear their footfalls. Also hand prints will appear, not on your trunk but on your bumper. There are two stories told to explain the phenomena. Two high school students heading home after the prom died when their car went off the road there. Now they just want to be alone and will push cars up the hill to get rid of intruders. In the other story, a bus load of children stalled at that spot. The children got out and tried to push it, but that bus rolled back down over them, killing them all.

MOORPARK

Moorpark is a city in Ventura County in Southern California. It is reported that a magnetic hill exist near Moorpark Community College near 12772 Kagel Canyon Road. In the 1940's, a school bus full of children broke down at that spot. The children got out and waited behind the bus for it to be fixed. A recklessly driving farmer ran into the back of the bus and killed the children. Another version says that a bus crashed when its brakes failed on the hill. All the children on the bus were killed. Both version s claim that the ghosts of the dead children now push vehicles up the hill to safety.

MORENO VALLEY

Moreno Valley is a city in Riverside County. A magnetic hill is said to exist on "Priest Hill" on Nason Street. One story says that a priest's car was broken down on the hill and he was killed when another vehicle hit him. Hence, the hill is called locally "Priest Hill". He supposedly pushes you up the hill to safety. Another story claims that a truck hit a bus loaded with kids that had broken down at that spot. Now the ghosts of the kids killed push your car up the hill. Whether the priest or the kids, you can see hand prints on the back of your vehicle if you put flour on it. Right. Sound familiar? Another story claims that there are two magnetic hills in Moreno Valley. One is on Nason street and the other is on "Priest Hill".

NORCO

I found a brief mention of a gravity hill on Mount Shasta Drive in Norco, a city in Riverside County, but I have been unable to find any further information.

NORTH RIDGE

There is reportedly a gravity hill in North Ridge, a neighborhood in Los Angeles in the San Fernando Valley. The directions are bit confusing but here they are. Take tampa Avenue off 118. Then two right turns after Rinaldi Street, you should crest a hill and go down the slope and stop. This should be the spot.

OCOTILLO

To get to the gravity hill in Ocotillo, drive down I-8 to the Mountain Springs exit and stop at the bottom of the off ramp.

If you are coming from the east on I-8, you will have to get off at Exit 87 head back to the Mountain Springs exit. You will appear to roll back up the ramp when you put it in neutral. Be very careful as this is an exit off a highway.

PENNGROVE

There is a gravity hill on Lichau Road in the community of Penngrove in Ventura County. It is sometimes identified as being in Rohnert Park. The spot is after a dip in the road at a small hill. Local legend says that the ghost of children killed years ago in a wagon accident will push your vehicle up the incline and also leave small hand prints on your trunk. Another story says it was a bus load of kids.

You can get to it from the Rohnert Park area on Redwood Highway (101) just south of Santa Rosa. Drive on the Rohnert Park Expressway east to Petaluma Hill Road where you take Petaluma Hill road south to Roberts Road. Follow Roberts Road east to Lichau Road where you follow it until you spot an iron gate with a sign saying``Gracias Santiago". You then drive to the bottom of the dip and stop.

Videos at
www.youtube.com/watch?v=IeyEZ9RZi7c&feature=related

www.youtube.com/watch?v=wUnPoZ2u_tA

SAN BERNARDINO

A gravity hill in the San Bernardino area can be experienced by driving north on Highway 18 towards Lake Arrowhead. You have to turn right on the old Waterman Canyon Road and drive until you see a small bridge. Next you drive onto the bridge, stop, put your car in neutral and it supposedly roll slowly up the hill. This is the first time I have heard of this phenomenon occurring on a bridge.

SAN DIEGO

The exit ramp in Mira Mesa/Sorrento Valley off 805-S is a gravity hill. Be careful if you try this as it is a freeway off ramp. They say to park your car at the bottom of the ramp and put your vehicle in neutral. Because of the way the road is made, it actually turns upward just a little bit at the very end of the ramp. There is supposedly another gravity hill on that highway but I would not recommend trying it as it is right on the interstate itself between the Descanso and the Willows Road exits. That stretch is apparently open to bicycles and those riders seem to be able to climb that hill with ease.

video at www.youtube.com/watch?v=S9VOjSueam0
www.youtube.com/watch?v=XrtuHMaCDHQ

Another gravity hill is also said to exist on Mountain Springs Road Exit 80 off the I-8 heading towards San Diego. There are urban legends about this spot being haunted but I have not as yet found any information on them.

I have seen a reference to a magnetic hill on the Sorrento Drive exit from Interstate 5 South but have found no further information.

SIERRA CANAL

Here is another different kind of magnetic hill only it is a canal. A Pacific Gas and Electric company canal crosses under Highway 20 about four miles west of the Interstate 80 junction in Placer County . To drivers traveling west on the highway, the water in the cannel appears to flow uphill. It is of course an optional illusion easily proved by placing a carpenter's level placed on the concrete canal's wall of the canal.

TAFT

A gravity hill is said to exist off Highway 33 in the oil fields between the small towns of Taft and Fellows. Look for a sign on Highway 33 that says Gravity Hill Road and take it to the south. After a short distance, you should see a sign that says you have reached Section 24B. There should be a hill at this spot. Park at the bottom facing north and put your car in neutral. Let me know how it turns out.

WHITTIER

Whittier is a suburb of Los Angeles in southern California. have you ever heard of a gravity hill in a cemetery? Rose Hills Cemetery, off Workman Mill Rd., near Rio Hondo Community College and the interchange of the 605 and 60 freeways in the Los Angeles suburb of Whittier is home to one. It is in the area with the rose gardens and burial vaults at the bottom of a small hill. I do not not recommend trying to test it as it is a cemetery. The cemetery employees also try to discourage thrill seekers.

Another gravity hill is apparently located on Turnbull Canyon Road in Whittier. This area is known for tales of Satanic cults and UFO sightings.

YUCAIPA

The gravity hill about ten miles or so down Oak Glen Road and two turns pass Riley's Farm is another one of those supposedly haunted spots. It was cursed by an old woman many considered a witch who lived nearby. A car load of teenagers died when their car crashed at that cursed spot and now their ghosts push your car up the hill to keep you from suffering the same fate.

FLORIDA

LAKE WALES

In public domain as per wikimapia.org/4493364/Spook-Hill#/photo/258951
licensed under the Creative Commons Attribution 3.0 Unported license.

Spook Hill lies on North Wales Drive, North Avenue, Lake Wales, Florida between Orlando and Tampa. It became famous when an article on it appeared on the front page of the Wall Street Journal on October 25, 1990, as well as being featured on CBS Morning News with Charles Osgood on November 5, 1990. The hill is next to Spook Hill Elementary School that adopted Casper The Friendly Ghost as their school mascot and is close to Bok Tower. Coordinates are 27°54'25"N 81°34'52"W

Video at
www.youtube.com/watch?v=fta_7O-Myms&NR=1
www.youtube.com/watch?v=Lkl5qhFaD3k&feature=related

GEORGIA

CUMMING

A haunted magnetic hill is located at Booger Hill a.k.a. Booger Mountain in Cumming, a city in Forsyth County. Be aware that ghosts from an old slave burial ground do not like visitors. When you park your car at the bottom of the hill and put it in neutral, they will pull it back up the hill. They even leave hand prints on your car. Some say you can even heard the spirits whispering. To get to the site, take Tribble Gap Road north out of town past Dr. Dunn road on your right and then drive past the two oak trees that are said to "hang over the road" from both directions. When you spy telephone poles running across at an 90 degree angle to Tribble Gap Road you are there. Stop beside the last telephone pole, supposedly the one right beside the road and put you car in neutral and see what happens.

FORT GAINES

Some call it Spook Hill while others call it Gravity Hill. It can be found two miles east of Highway 39 on Days Cross Road north of the town of Fort Gaines in southwest Georgia . You have to cross CR 50. Stop at the curve sign at the bottom of the hill. Make sure you are facing west and that should be the spot. Another set of instructions say it is on County Road 135, one and seven-tenths miles from Days Crossroads.

MANCHESTER

A magic hill once existed about one mile out of Manchester, a city in Meriwether and Talbot Counties. It was once a tourist attraction on private land but is now apparently torn down. It was supposedly torn down. But one investigator claims that the hill is still there but is overgrown. It is not recommenced venturing on this site without permission of the owner.

IDAHO

CULDESAC

Culdesac is a town in Nez Perce County and has a gravity hill of its own. It is located on Culdesac Road (Culdesac Grade) west out of town. About half way on the grade there is a spot that looks apparently looks like it is uphill but actually is going down towards the town.

INDIANA

MOORESVILLE

Mooresville in Morgan County has a gravity hill on Keller Hill Road off State Road 42 on the south side of the town. If you wish to see it, drive west out of town on High Street which is two blocks south of Main. High Street turns into State Road 24. At the first right take Keller Hill Road and drive approximately one mile crossing several small hills. When you come to the big hill you should see a silo just before the spot. Line up your car at a big old tree on the right if it is still there and put your car in neutral. Enjoy the experience. Once again, the explanation for the phenomenon is that of a school bus that stalled at the bottom of the hill at the railway tracks and was struck by a train. The ghosts of the children killed now push cars stopped at that spot out of danger. The story also suggests sprinkling flour on the truck and finger prints will appear.

KENTUCKY

COVINGTON

Covington is a city in Kenton County at the confluence of the Ohio and Licking rivers. There is a gravity hill in Ridgeway Court near Devou Park in Covington. To get to it, you have to drive through Devou Park until you see River Hill St. Then drive uphill on River Hill Street until it turns sharply to the right into Ridgeway Court. Look for a high cement wall and a line of telephone poles on the left and stop at the second pole. This should be the spot. Be respectful of the neighborhood residents and watch for traffic.

Pictures available at www.roadsideamerica.com/tip/35103

PRINCETON

There is a haunted gravity hill on a side road to the right at some railroad tracks about one mile west of Princeton. It is said that if you stop or stall on or near those tracks, you car will be pushed up hill to safety by unseen hands. There are two stories that tell who it is that is doing the pushing. In the early's 1950's, a woman was raped and murdered near that spot. Now is is believed that her ghost is trying to push vehicles out of the way before her killer returns. The other story claims that a bus load of children were killed at that spot when the bus stalled on the tracks and was hit by a train. Their ghosts are trying to push cars to safety. You decided which story is right. To get to the hill, take Highway 91 through Princeton pass Walmart towards Eddyville. When you see the first sign for the Eddyville Prison, turn right and you should be there.

MARYLAND

BURKITTSVILLE

Spook Hill is located on Gapland Road just outside Burkittsville, Frederick County. To check it out, take West

Main Street/Gapland Road from the downtown square of Burkkittsville to the northwest until you drive up a hill with a large red barn on the left. Go to the bottom of the hill. This should be the spot. Local legend claims that the ghosts of Confederate soldiers killed in a Civil War battle are pushing vehicles up the hill perhaps thinking that they were cannon.

Video for Burritsville at
www.youtube.com/watch?v=ZHPmdO_f-wI&feature=related

OWINGS MILLS

There is another Spook Hill on Ward's Chapel Road through Soldier's Delight Park near Owings Mill, a suburb of Baltimore, in Baltimore County.

Its Coordinates are 39.4166016, -76.84468746

MASSACHUSETTS

GREENFIELD

Greenfield is a city in Franklin County and has a gravity hill on Shelburne Road as one of its attractions. To try this site out Exit 26 off I-91 and head west on Highway 2. Make an right on Colrain Road and then a left on Shelburne Road. Drive through the Highway 2 underpass and make a u-turn. Stop your car by the white road marker that is about one hundred and fifty feet east of the underpass on the left side of the road. This should be the spot. Remember to observe all safety rules listed earlier in this book.

HARVARD

Harvard is a town in Worcester County and is located twenty-five miles west-northwest of Boston, in eastern Massachusetts. Its gravity hill starts on a flat spot at 38 Stow Road, next to the mailbox. When you park at this spot you supposedly can see the incline ahead at the second curve in the street.

LEOMINSTER

There is or was a gravity hill on Lowe Street on the southwest edge of the town of Leominster in Worcester County. The street is about a half a mile long and can be found several blocks south of Barrett and runs west from Pleasant Street. It was reported on www.roadsideamerica.com/tip/15439 that the gravity hill is gone but I am not sure what that means.

MICHIGAN

ARCADIA TOWNSHIP

There is a gravity hill a few miles north of Arcadia Township in Manistee County. Drive north on Highway M22 from Arcadia until you come to Joyfield Road. Take a right and drive until you see Blaine Church. Here you turn right on Putney Road and proceed a few hundred yards until you are at the bottom of a hill. You are now in Benzie County. You have arrived at the gravity hill.

Map at www.eureka4you. com/magnetichillworldwide/Arcadia-MI.htm
Video at www.youtube.com/watch?v=IdMIwkO_vwM

ROSE CITY

Rose City has a magnetic hill past Heath Road at the end of Reasoner Road . Directions suggest that you drive east from the stoplight on 33 in Rose City. Go about three miles and turn left on Reasoner Road so that you are heading north. You should cross Heath Road several miles further on. Reasoner Road ends on a curve at the top of a hill. This is the magnetic hill.

Map and Photos are at
www.eureka4you.com/magnetichillworldwide/RoseCity-MI.htm

ST. IGNACE

Three California surveyors, while working in the northern peninsula in the 1950's in Michigan, discovered a spot at 150 Martin Lake Road, St. Ignace. Their surveying equipment did not seem to work properly on this piece of land. Using a plum -bob or bubble level to level their tripod, the bubble level level but the plump-bob always swung to the east. This mystery spot became famous and you can find more information on their website at www.mysteryspotstignace.com/ www.mysteryspotstignace.com/

MISSOURI

FREEMAN

A gravity hill can be found at the intersection of State Highway D and East 299th Street southwest of town just outside of Louisburg, near the Kansas border.

MONTANA

DEER LODGE

A gravity hill exists just outside Deer Lodge, a city in and the county seat of Powell County. I am not sure but it could be on Boulder River Road as a poster suggested on youtube when they view the videos at

www.youtube. com/watch?v=QCbqV2bXS5Q&feature=related and www.youtube.com/watch?v=p9DreSlV9MQ

NEW JERSEY

FRANKLIN LAKES

Franklin Lakes is a borough in Bergen County. A gravity road has been reported on Ewing Avenue. The exit ramp from Highway 208 to Ewing Ave is the gravity road or hill. I suggest that you do not test it out. It is a busy road and it is against the law for any vehicle to back up on an off-ramp. The police will ticket you. According to local legend, a young woman killed at that spot will push your car back up the ramp when you stop at the stop sign. They even say you can find her hand prints on your front bumper by putting some sort of powder on it. I though the ghost would push on your hood unless of course they were on their knees while pushing.

HOLMDEL

There is a gravity hill in Holmdel near Middletown in Monmouth County. It is on a hill just down the side street from the huge Lilly Tulip Plant on Highway 35. At the stop sign, if you put your car in neutral, you will appear to roll right up the hill.

JACKSON

There is a gravity hill at 1005 Farmingdale Road in Jackson. Experience Nightmare at Gravity Hill on the Cicconi Farm. What is Nightmare at Gravity Hill? Check out their website at nightmareatgravityhill.com/welcome.html

Also check out videos at the NightmateGravityHill's Channel at
www.youtube.
com/user/NightmareGravityHill/feed?feature=context

MORRIS TOWNSHIP

Magnetic Hill on Sussex Turnpike in Morris Township has been known for over one hundred years. The location is said to be at the entrance to the Bradford and Butterworth housing developments. Local legend says that inventor Thomas Edison developed a special formula that he poured on the road, and the remains of this special potion created the magnetic force. Apparently the road ha been re-graded and re-paved and the magnetic effect is now very small or nonexistent.

TITUSVILLE

The Titusville Gravity Road is off Pleasant Valley Road, off Route 29, along the Delaware-Raritan Canal between Trenton and Lambertville. Drive about a mile or so on it until you see a small sign on your left which tells you where to stop. Or stop at the stop sign at the bottom of a hill. There are two local legends told about this spot. One concerns the ghost of a farmer who came home one night and found his family trapped in their burning house. Unable to get in, he took a lantern out to the road where he found people watching the place burn. No one would help him. He rushed back and into the burning structure and he and all his family died. Now they say that he appears on the road at that spot with a lantern and will push or pull your car up the hill as he does not like people stopping there. Ghost lights have been reported at that spot.

A second legend claims that the ghost of a man, who was killed by a rapist when he tried to protect his daughter from the killer, is still trying to stop people from coming there. He supposedly is trying to push cars as far away from his house as he can. His and his daughter lived in a house five lots down the road to the right of the stop sign at the bottom of the hill.

There is also another gravity hill about two miles further on on Pleasant Valley Road near Titusville and Hopewell.

NEW YORK

ARKWRIGHT

A magnetic hill is said to be located in the town of Arkwright, a town in Chautauqua County. No details are available at the time of writing.

BRISTOL

The ghosts of an Indian Tribe are said to push cars uphill on an unspecified road in Bristol, a town in Ontario County.

MIDDLESEX

Spook Hill lies on Newell Road east of Canandaigua Lake in Middlesex. Twenty five years ago, a University of Rochester scientist check the phenomenon out and found that is was like all the others - an optical illusion.

NEW YORK CITY

It has been reported that there is a gravity hill on a back street between Wellsville and Olean in New York City but I have not been able to uncover any details.

PORTVILLE

A gravity road is supposedly located on Promised Land Road in Portville, a town in Cattaraugus County. I have not been able to find any more information on it.

Video at

www.youtube.com/watch?v=1-kLZZLQEg8

www.youtube.com/watch?v=lIwRSpbisG8&feature=related

OHIO

MENTOR

The gravity hill on King Memorial Road in the Kirtland Hills/Mentor area has no stories or legend attached to it. Apparently there have been a number of accidents at that spot so be careful when checking it out. To get to it you have to drive south on Little Mountain Road from Mentor Avenue or Old Johnnycake Ridge Road a few miles until you reach the King Memorial intersection which is a four way stop. Take a left on King Memorial Road.

Video at www.youtube.com/watch?v=akB_7qfyoew

OKLAHOMA

BARTLESVILLE

There is a gravity hill on Gap Road between Bartlesville and Ochelata. Local legend claims that a lot of slaves were hung there years ago. Their ghosts apparently push your car up hill.

The legend also warns that if you let them push it pass some railroad tracks you will die!

Video at www.youtube.com/watch?v=JSd_RoIlwkA

SPRINGER

What the locals call Magnetic Hill is located on Pioneer Road just one and one-half miles from Springer in west Oklahoma. Drive on Highway 53 to Pioneer Road and turn north. Go about one half mile to the bottom of the hill and you should be at the spot.

There are three photos at
www.OklahomaHistory.net/ttphotos/maghill2.jpg
www.OklahomaHistory.net/ttphotos/maghill3.jpg
www.OklahomaHistory.net/ttphotos/maghill4.jpg

The first picture looks north on Pioneer road to Vermont Road. The other two look south toward Highway 53 in northern Carter County near I-35 and Exit 42.

There is a map to Magnetic Hill www.OklahomaHistory. net/ttphotos/magmap.jpg GPS 34.3452   97.1780

YouTube Video at

www.youtube.com/watch?v=g_S64depdVE

www.oklahomahistory.net/magnetichill.html

PENNSYLVANIA

BUCKINGHAM TOWNSHIP

There is a hard to find gravity hill on Holicong Road in Bucks County about a quarter mile from the Mount Gilead African Methodist Episcopal Church. just before Buckingham Mountain. It is reportedly across the street and around the bend from the grave yard.

Video at www.youtube.com/watch?v=d7ED1yB7lHY

done to here

HARRISBURG

The city of Harrisburg , York County, has its own gravity hill on Pleasantview Road (Pleasant View Road) at State Route 177. To get to it, take Interstate 83 out of Harrisburg towards York. Take Exit 24 (Lewisberrry - Route 177) until you cross a small creek. Then turn right on Pleasantview Road. The gravity hill starts at the 177 and Pleasantview intersection where the white mark is at the stop sign on Pleasantview

Road. Your car should be facing Route 177. Remember all the safety suggestion mentioned earlier before putting your car in neutral.

Map and picture at www.eureka4you.com/magnetichillworldwide/Harrisburg-PA.htm

DANVILLE

Danville is a borough in Montour County. Several internet sites mention that Danville has a gravity hill but provide no information.

NEW PARIS

Image showed as in public domain as per Google.com

New Paris is a community near Schellsburg in Bedford County. This area has the distinction of having not just one but two gravity hills and on the same road separated by only three tenths of a mile. To experience this phenomena, take

Route 30 to the town of Schellsburg about eight miles west of Bedford. In Schellsburg, turn north at the only traffic light and drive north on Route 96 towards New Paris for about four miles. There is a small metal bridge just before New Paris. Take a left on Bethel Hollow Road or S.R 4016 and bear left at the "Y" in the road. There is an intersection about one and one half mile with a stop sign for on coming traffic. Turn right onto this road and look for the letters "GH" spray painted on the road. The second GH is about one tenth of a mile. If these directions are confusing or incorrect, there is a phone number listed on the internet (800) 765-3331 that apparently you can call for information.

Video at www.youtube.com/watch?v=2LawmLgSSRY
www.youtube.
com/watch?v=UUSDMPmo56U&feature=related

NURMIDIA

There is a gravity hill on Route 42 at Numidia which is is twenty two miles away from Berwick and one mile south of Slabtown.

Video at www.youtube.com/watch?v=sGmk5XAPlMU

TENNESSEE

CROSSVILLE

Crossville is a city in and the county seat of Cumberland County. There is apparently another haunted road and hill at Mile Marker Ten on Interstate 40. Years ago, a bus with kids broke down on the slope of the hill and a tractor trailer coming fast over the crest crashed into the bus killing everyone on it. Now if you put your vehicle in neutral when you get to the hill, the ghosts of the children will push you up and over the crest to safety and out of the way of oncoming traffic. And when you check the back of your car, you will find the hand prints of the ghostly children on the truck. Or so they say! But remember the road is busy and you hazard an accident if you try this stunt.

JOHNSON CITY

The Okolona road exit in Johnson City in Washington County is another one of those haunted magnetic hills you hear about from time to time. The story goes that if you stop on the exit, put your car in neutral, it will start rolling up the incline. The local explanation says that your car is being pushed by the ghosts of two people killed when their car stalled on the exit and was hit by another car. They say that you can sometimes see the imprints of their hands on car's back windows. The ghosts do not want you to suffer their fate. One good way to make sure you do not, is to NOT STOP on that exit.

TEXAS

EL PASO

There is a gravity or magnetic hill at 820 Thunderbird Drive between Twin Hills Drive and Singing Hills Drive.

SAN ANTONIO

In San Antonio, you can find a gravity hill at the railway crossing at Villamain Road and Shane Road just east of the San Antonio Missions National Historic Park on the southeastern edge of the city. Supposedly the ghosts of children killed at that spot will push your vehicle almost thirty feet up the slight hill and onto railroad tracks! To get to its, take exit 42 off I-410 and turn south onto Southton Road. Then take the second right onto Shane Road and look for the railroad tracks. Be careful as these tracks are still in use.

The SyFy show "FACT OR FAKED" investigated this gravity hill and concluded that it is an optical illusion.

A map showing its location is available at
www.roadsideamerica.com/map/1298

UTAH

SALT LAKE CITY

Kristin Payne chases spare tire "uphill" on gravity hill as | belief from "downhill" pointed car. Engineers explain the
Jean Miskin and Rearitz (Chris) Christensen look in dis- | illusion comes from different ascendancy rates of hill, road.

Gravity Hill, Salt Lake City, Utah, in Public Domain as per Google.com

Gravity Hill, Salt Lake City, Utah, Today. Said to be in Public Domain as per Google.com

A magnetic hill exists a few blocks northeast of the Capitol building in Salt Lake City. You used to be able to get to it by driving up past the east side of the capitol building, and look for Bonneville Blvd. It looped around a park in lower City Creek Canyon called Memory Grove. In February of 2007, the gravity hill was apparently closed to two way traffic. To get to it now you have drive on North Temple to State Street, turn on to 2nd. Ave and go up the hill to B St. Here you turn left up the hill to 11th Ave. and then straight to Bonneville Blvd to the new entrance in the canyon is called City Creek Canyon.

There are two different stories that reputedly explain the gravity reversal. A man driving a tractor up the hill died when the tractor tipped over on the hill and he fell. Now he tries to save others by pushing their vehicle to safety. The other story claims that the nearby grave of a man named Emo is responsible for the amazing effect. Oh yes! Emo's grave glows blue at midnight.

A map of the location is at www.roadsideamerica. com/map/1833.

Other photos may still be available at

www.examiner.com/slideshow/gravity-hill-salt-lake-city-utah#slide=3

www.examiner.com/slideshow/gravity-hill-salt-lake-city-utah#slide=2

VIRGINIA

DANVILLE

A witch was said to have once lived in an old abandoned house close to the intersection of Oak Hill Road and Berry Hill Road just west of Danville in Pittsylvania County. Her spirit is said to draw people to her house. If you stop at the stop sign at that intersection and put your vehicle in neutral it will start to roll backwards. There does not appear to be an incline there but it does exist. Be careful that there are no cars behind you when you try this.

www.forgottenus.com/index.php?p=place.view&place=1963

WASHINGTON

PROSSER

About ten miles east of the community of Prosser in Benton County near a small farm, there is a haunted gravity hill. There is supposed to be a spot where the words "START" are painted on the road. Put you car in neutral after taking all the recommenced precautions and your vehicle will start rolling "uphill". Local legend claims that the ghost of a girl raped in a nearby barn is pushing it up the hill. Another version says that the girl's ghost comes out of a dried up canal where she drown years ago and pushes your car. The usual fingerprints of the ghost will appear if you put powder on the trunk of you automobile.

WEST VIRGINIA

LOGAN

Years ago a woman was killed and her body was found on 22 Mountain Mine Road at Logan. Now, local legend claims that if you stop your car at that spot and put it in neutral, the ghost of the dead woman will push it up the hill. It is actually an optical illusion and the up incline is , of course, a down slope.

WISCONSIN

SHULLSBURG

Gravity Hill lies near White's Hill just south just south of Rennick Road, on County Truck U, south of Shullsburg, in LaFayette County, Wisconsin. Approximately two miles out of town, the highway drops down a steep hill, and heads back up a steeper hill. Stop your car just short of the 25 mph sign facing back up the hill. This should be the spot. Remember to be cautious as there is traffic on this road.

Map at www.eureka4you.com/magnetichillworldwide/Shullsburg-WI.htm

Hand drawn map from Wisconsin State Journal, July 18, 1994

STOCKBRIDGE

Joe Road, listed as "Joe's Road" on a number of web sites, lies three miles (five kilometers) south of Stockbridge west off STH 55.95. There is a local story that a cemetery grounds keeper names Indian Joe was killed and buried under a new road that was being built through an old Indian Burial Ground in the early 1900's. He apparently protested the road. Supposedly there is no evidence that Indian Joe and the Indian Burial ground existed. Why am I telling you this? Well, local legend says that if you drive down Joe's Road, which runs "uphill both ways", stopping at the bottom and putting you car in neutral, Indian Joe will push it up the hill. He does not like anyone stopping over the Indian Burial ground. If you do not believe this story, then put powder or flour on the car's trunk and you will find what people say are Joe's finger prints. There is a logical explanation for fingerprints on the trunk. Any one who closes it will leave them and the prints can last a long time - even after the vehicle has been washed. Take a look at a topographical map of the area and you will see it shows the supposed upslope is actually a seventy foot long downward incline.

APPENDIX A
AN ALTERNATE THEORY

Sing H. Lin, Ph.D has investigated many mystery spots and believes that the magnetic abnormalities are real and not the result of illusion. In his abstract, "My 20 Year Work", he explains that tests and measurements done by people at these sites to prove they are illusions are not valid proofs because of defects in the testing and equipment used that he observed while studying the reports. He purposes that the strange gravity phenomena on gravity hills and at mystery spots may be real and not due to illusion. He further suggest that the gravitational effect may be due to "dark matter" that scientists think exist and are now investigating.

REFERENCES

INTERNET

ankurlearningsolutions.wordpress.com/2013/11/19/magnetic-hill-near-leh-in- ladakh-india/

answers.yahoo.com/question/index?qid=20080816124348AAuGHR7

www.sonomastatestar.com/features/rohnert-park-s-mystery-gravity-hill-   1.1472839#.Uv-xPYUz34w

atriptoireland.com/2013/03/21/the-magic-roads-of-ireland/

bucks.happeningmag.com/search-for-gravity-hill-buckingham/

en.wikipedia.org/wiki/Ayrshire Electric Brae

en.wikipedia.org/wiki/Electric_Brae

en.wikipedia.org/wiki/Epping_Forest.49

en.wikipedia.org/wiki/FileOrroroo,_Magnetic_Hill.JPG

en.wikipedia.org/wiki/Kur%C5%A1umlija.43

en.wikipedia.org/wiki/List_of_gravity_hills

en.wikipedia.org/wiki/Magnetic_Hill_Area_Moncton

en.wikipedia.org/wiki/Oak_Grove

en.wikipedia.org/wiki/Polo,_Barahona El Polo Magnético

en.wikipedia.org/wiki/Radan_Mountain

en.wikipedia.org/wiki/Spook_Hill

en.wikipedia.org/w/index.php?title=Hangman 27s_Hill&action=edit&redlink=1

en.wikipedia.org/wiki/Wonder_Spot

findery.com/places/541447203420

www.gravityhill.com/

groups.yahoo. com/neo/groups/ontroads/conversations/topics/7367

gstcjourney.blogspot.com/2010/09/machakos-water-runs-uphill-and-cars.html

hasnainhayder.tripod.com/

kielyscomments.tripod.com/places.htm

news.okezone.com/read/2011/04/17/340/447003/wow-ada-jabal-magnet
-di-   banyumas
pacabinsandcottages.com/southwestern_attractions.html
paranormal.about.com/library/blstory_december02_08.htm
schwarze.com/top-10-most-unusual-streets-to-sweep/
userpages.umbc.edu/~frizzell/gravhills.html
weirdnj.com/stories/gravity-roads/
wikimapia.org/4493364/Spook-Hill
www.academia.edu/4701453/Antigravity_Hills_are_Visual_Illusions
www.angelfire.com/weird2/georgia/page3.html
www.atlasobscura.com/places/mooresvilles-gravity-hill
www.b92.net/info/vesti/index.php?
www.b92.net/info/vesti/index.php?
                    yyyy=2010&mm=08&dd=04&nav_id=449862
wwww.burlingtonghostwalks.ca/burlingtonghosts3.htm
www.cicap.org/lazio/temp.php?d=6&a=25
www.cicap.org/piemonte/cicap.php?section=indagini_in&content=salite
www.cosmosmysteryarea.com/history.html
www.ehow.com/list_5996855_west-georgia-
attractions.html#ixzz2tPveeOtVwww.eureka4you.com/magnetichill/
www.eureka4you.com/magnetichillworldwide/Arcadia-MI.htm
www.eureka4you.com/magnetichillworldwide/Dacre-ON.htm
www.eureka4you.com/magnetichillworldwide/Harrisburg-PA.htm
www.eureka4you.com/magnetichillworldwide/Helena-AR.htm
www.eureka4you.com/magnetichillworldwide/LakeWales-FL.htm
www.eureka4you.com/magnetichillworldwide/LosBanos-LA.htm
www.eureka4you.com/magnetichillworldwide/Moonbi-NSW.htm
www.eureka4you.com/magnetichillworldwide/Mooresville-IN.htm
www.eureka4you.com/magnetichillworldwide/NewParis-PA.htm
www.eureka4you.com/magnetichillworldwide/Peterborough-SA.htm
www.eureka4you.com/magnetichillworldwide/Princeton-KY.htm
www.eureka4you.com/magnetichillworldwide/Richmond-NSW.htm
www.eureka4you.com/magnetichillworldwide/RohnertPark-CA.htm
www.eureka4you.com/magnetichillworldwide/RoseCity-MI.htm
www.examiner.com/topic/optical-illusion/articles
www.examiner.com/article/challenge-your-perception-at-la-jolla-s-
gravity-hill
www.examiner.com/topic/la-jolla gravity hill
www.experienceproject.com/stories/Paranormal-Investigator/286554
www.forteantimes.com/features/articles/175/gravity_anomalies.html
www.fqxi.org/community/forum/topic/868

www.ghosttraveller.com/missouri.htm
www.hauntedrooms.co.uk/epping-forest-essex
www.hindu.com/thehindu/2003/06/07/stories/2003060706450300.htm
harvard.wickedlocal.com/x721532271
www.lifeinthefingerlakes.com/articles.php?view=article&id=324
www.liminality.org/imagery/jeju2005/48/
www.magnetichill.com/english.htm
www.manxforums.com/forums/index.php?/topic/10806-where-is/
www.mcintyre.demon.co.uk/local/electbrae.htm
www.mysteryhill-nc.com
www.mysteryhill-nc.com/#!history-of-mystery-hill/c1uho
www.mysteryspotstignace.com/
www.newryjournal.co.uk/2004/05/10/gravity-hills/
www.news10.net/news/article/145433/2/Gravity-defied--Sierra-canal-appears-to-flow-uphill
www.odeaanaude.eu/catalog/-p-663.html
www.oregonvortex.com/
www.pasadenaviews.com/day-16-of-365-gravity-hill/
www.peterboroughsa.com.au/magnetic.php
www.research.umbc.edu/%7Efrizzell/gravhills.html
www.roadsideamerica.com/tip/327
www.roadsideamerica.com/tip/874
www.roadsideamerica.com/map/3300
www.roadsideamerica.com/tip/3303
www.roadsideamerica.com/tip/14577
www.roadsideamerica.com/tip/15871
www.roadsideamerica.com/tips/getAttraction.php?tip_AttractionNo==1298
www.roadsideamerica.com/tips/getAttraction.php?tip_AttractionNo==1796
www.roadsideamerica.com/tips/getAttraction.php?tip_AttractionNo==1833 www.roadsideamerica.com/tips/getAttraction.php?tip_AttractionNo==3300
www.roadsideamerica.com/tips/getAttraction.php?tip_AttractionNo==6523. www.roadsideamerica.com/location/tx
www.roadsideamerica.com/location/ut
www.roadsideamerica.com/set/SCIspots.html
www.sandiegoreader.com/news/2013/feb/13/straight-gravity-hill/
www.sdparanormal.com/articles/article/764209/5942.htm
www.sdparanormal.com/articles/article/764209/5942.htm#sthash.9VcwRT1U.dpuf

www.standardmedia.co.ke/?articleID=2000068488
www.strangeusa.com/ViewLocation.aspx?locationid=10528
www.taringa.net/posts/apuntes-y-monografias/4135417/El-Paso-
Misterioso-   donde-las-cosas-bajan-la-subida.html
www.thewideawakecafe.com/?cat=51
www.tourismvernon.com/index.php/tourism-services/visitor-centre/
www.travelchinaguide.com/cityguides/liaoning/shenyang/
www.unexplainedresearch.com/files_anomalies/wonder_spot.html
www.usatoday.com/travel/news/2007-02-05-wonder-spot_x.htm.
www.waymarking.
com/waymarks/WM6TPG_Gravity_Hill_at_Devou_Park_Covington_K
Y
www.waymarking.
com/waymarks/WMCXAY_Gravity_Hill_Road_near_Moravska_Trebo
va_Czech_Republic
www.weirdnj.com/index.php?
weirdus.com/states/ohio/road_less_traveled/gravity_hill/index.
phpwesclark.com/jw/spook_hill.html

OTHER

Bressan, Paola, Antigravity Hills are Visual Illusion
Cross, Patrick, Burlington Post and Hamilton Spectator Newspaper
articles-1985,2003,2005,2008)
Haughton, Brian, Haunted Spaces, Sacred Places: A Field Guide to
Stone Circles, Crop Circles
Jacobs, Linda, "Big Pull News Article, August 16th, 1985"

PICTURES

www.examiner.com/slideshow/gravity-hill-salt-lake-city-utah#slide=2

www.examiner.com/slideshow/gravity-hill-salt-lake-city-utah#slide=3

YouTube websites of interest:

www.youtube.com/watch?v=jd0A4bnp-YU&feature=related Unknown location

youtube.com/watch?v=D7cV32S3s_0&feature=related on the Isle of Man

ABOUT THE AUTHOR

James Foster Robinson was born in Ogdensburg, New York, USA but grew up in Prescott, Ontario, Canada. He has lived and worked in Ontario, Manitoba, Alberta and . In 2005, he moved to West Virginia and married his present wife, Betty. Jim has two books published by Mika Publishing, Belleville, Ontario Amazing Tales from Eastern Ontario, 1987; Strange But True Tales From Eastern Ontario, 1989. He has also published numerous articles in national magazines, daily and weekly newspapers. While living in Vancouver, BC, Jim was a Feature Writer on Suite101.com for topics - The Art of Storytelling, Storyteller's Korner, Sleep Disorders, Professional Security, and Liechtenstein. In addition, he was a

Storyteller both in Kingston, Ontario and in Vancouver, BC, Canada. James has also published "A Ghostly Guide to West Virginia", "West Virginia Weird and Wonderful", "An Encyclopedia of Lake and River Monsters", "Riotous Times, An Unauthorized History of Riots and Violent Protests in British Columbia, Canada", "A Ghostly Guide to Kentucky", "A Ghostly Guide to California", "The Wampus Cat, Myth or Reality", "Sleep Dancing With Death/Struggling with Sleep Apnea", "Storytelling for Fun", "Are They Ghosts?", "British Columbia Weird" and a children book "Tales To Tell My Children", a novel "Umpock - The Hole In The Ground", and his latest book "Ghost Lights, Spook Lights, Will o' Wisps and Friends" on Amazon.com. He is presently working on Ghostly Guides to the remaining 46 states and the 10 provinces of Canada.

www.ingramcontent.com/pod-product-compliance
Lightning Source LLC
Chambersburg PA
CBHW051945280526
45789CB00009B/3175

* 9 7 8 1 4 9 9 5 3 5 6 4 8 *